6 Ways
We Encounter God

Leader Guide

6 Decisions
That Will Change Your Life

Participant Workbook
DVD
Leader Guide

6 Things
We Should Know About God

Participant Workbook
DVD
Leader Guide

6 Ways
We Encounter God

Participant Workbook
DVD
Leader Guide

6 Ways

We Encounter God

Leader Guide

Tom Berlin

with Karen Berlin and Becky Kendall

Abingdon Press
Nashville

Six Ways We Encounter God
Leader Guide

Tom Berlin with Karen Berlin and Becky Kendall

Copyright © 2014 by Abingdon Press
All rights reserved.

This book is printed on acid-free, elemental chlorine-free paper.

ISBN 978-1-426-79470-4

14 15 16 17 18 19 20 21 22 23—10 9 8 7 6 5 4 3 2 1
MANUFACTURED IN THE UNITED STATES OF AMERICA

Contents

Introduction

Six Ways We Encounter God is a six-week small group experience that gives participants an opportunity to learn about different qualities of God's character and discuss the ways they are encountering God in their daily lives. The group will meet weekly to watch a video and complete Scripture study that will describe aspects of God's holiness, providing new perspectives into the character of God. The common goal of the Participant Workbook, DVD, and this Leader Guide is to provide an opportunity to look closely at the character of God and gain fresh insights into the character that God wants to form in each of us.

Covenant Formation

It is important that each group function out of a set of shared values. Coming to a consensus or a "covenant" about what group members can anticipate from their small group will help set a tone of trust and mutuality. It is important that each member knows the small group is a safe environment to share personal information. You are encouraged to make confidentiality a part of your group covenant.

How to Use This Leader Guide

Each group will meet for six weeks for the purpose of discussing and putting into practice lessons learned during the week from the Participant Workbook. Your group can tailor the activities and discussion to the time available, usually ranging from 60 to 90 minutes with the majority of that time spent in small group discussion.

The session format described in this guide is designed to aid you as leader and facilitator and to help guide the small group experience. Sessions are easily adaptable for groups that meet for varying lengths of time. Leaders can use the sessions as they are written or choose from among the various components offered, as described below.

Preparing

A brief summary is provided at the beginning of each session so you can begin with an overview and understanding of the main goal of each week's lesson. Knowing the intended goal for the session will enable you to pick questions and manage your time within the small group to be sure the main points are discussed.

Icebreakers and Conversation Starters

Opener options have been included for each session. These activities and conversation starters help your group members connect in a fun, informal manner before entering a time of more personal and reflective sharing. Choose only one activity from the options offered. If your group meets for less than 90 minutes, you may opt to use an opener activity in the first week only, when group members may be meeting for the first time, then forgo openers in the weeks after.

The activities that are included relate in some way to the imagery used in the video or discussion topic, but you are certainly free to select what you think will work best for your group, and you may opt for an alternative opener of your own choosing.

Logistics and Covenant

At your first group meeting, you may want to take time to share important logistical information relevant to your group. This may encompass things such as parking, childcare concerns, start time, discussion format, shared leadership roles, cell phone usage, refreshments, and potential scheduling conflicts.

This is also the time to form and agree on a group covenant: a set of guidelines for behavior in the sessions and mutual promises to respect one another, listen to one another, and treat personal information shared in the group as confidential.

Workbook Review

Encourage group members to bring their Participant Workbooks to each meeting. Each session includes an opportunity for them to share reflections and insights gained from reading the workbook, studying the Scriptures, and writing down their thoughts.

Your group will find that responding to the daily readings and workbook questions will greatly enhance their experience in this study and enrich the group session. Though some group members may not be keeping up in the Participant Workbook, you'll want to include this review portion of the session for those who are doing it. Allowing this time for sharing will not only reinforce those who are practicing this discipline but will also allow others to benefit from other group members' insights and experiences.

Show DVD Video

The DVD includes a 4-5 minute video to "hook" the participants and launch the small group discussion each week. A metaphor is embedded within each video to provide a unique means to consider the specific theme of each session. In addition to the imagery, the video contains an introduction or tie-in to the Scripture passage that will be studied. Finally, each video ends with a question to which group members will share their responses.

Video Discussion

This section provides questions to discuss immediately following the video presentation, to assist group members in considering the imagery, metaphors, and stories used in the video. These questions serve as meaningful segues into the Scripture and Discussion section that will follow.

Scripture and Discussion

This is the most critical and constant component of each session. The session will focus on the Bible passages for that session that are included in the Participant Workbook. Each session will list a Scripture passage to be read aloud and then offer a variety of questions for review, reflection, and personal application.

Note that the sequence and number of questions is up to you and your group, and if desired you may decide to generate your own questions. Those completing the Participant Workbook will have read additional Scriptures during the week, and you are welcome to draw upon those selections to add to the study and discussion of the topic. Whichever questions you decide to use, you are strongly encouraged to include some of the questions with personal-application value that are listed toward the end of each section.

Closing

A closing prayer has been included for each session for those who wish to use it. You may choose to use the prayer listed simply as a resource or not at all. How your prayer is structured and offered is left to the discretion of you and your group. The prayer may be led by you, by another group member, or by the entire group. Sharing of joys and concerns should be included in the closing prayer.

Notes

A section of blank lines is provided at the end of each week's lesson. This space allows you to make notes that will assist you as you lead your small group. It can also be used to insert times, prayer requests, and other relevant information.

God's Majesty
and My Reverence

God's Majesty and My Reverence

Preparing

The goal of this week's session is to evoke reverence for the holiness of God as the divine grandeur, majesty, and glory are considered. Contemplating the magnificent wonders of God's handiwork helps individuals get into the proper perspective concerning God. When we are awed by God, we realize how great God is and how small we are by comparison. Experiencing an overwhelming sense of God's greatness allows the modern-day disciple of Christ to place God, rather than one's own life, in the center of the universe.

The video elicits reverence through the examination of one of God's least likely creatures, the slug. By focusing on the purpose, function, and unique nature of the slug, reverence for the genius and creativity of its Creator is inspired. Similarly, contemplating the slug helps viewers consider how vast and great must be God's love for them. If the caretaker of the universe was willing to invest so much thought and care to craft the existence of a slug, how deep and unending must be God's love for us as well.

Psalm 104 was selected for extra examination to focus participants' attention upon the mystery, wonder, and grandeur of all creation. Discussion questions are designed to help modern-day disciples find humility before God and seek and experience a relationship of reverence and worship with the Lord.

Getting Started

As this is the first week of a new study for your group, it is important to allow adequate time for introductions. Even if most of your group members are familiar with one another, using an icebreaker will strengthen connections and will be of great benefit to even one newcomer present. In addition to providing name tags for the group, consider choosing one of the following openers to let your group get to know one another and prepare for their time together.

Icebreakers (choose one)

1. **Something Few People Know About Me:** Ask members to introduce themselves and share one fact about themselves that is little known.

2. **Favorites:** Ask each member to respond to a "Favorites" question, such as favorite movie, food, dessert, book, vacation spot, song, hobby, job, color, and so on.

3. **Categorical Descriptors:** Choose a category, such as cars, sports, food, or shoes, and ask each member to name an object within that category that may describe them. Examples: one person might be a pair of spikes because they like to dig deep into things; another might choose a slipper because it offers warmth and comfort; someone else might name fajitas because they are full of zest and spice; another might choose milk because it is wholesome and familiar.

4. **Motion Name Game:** Have the members of your group introduce themselves by saying their names and demonstrating motions to go with them. As each group member offers her or his name, the entire group responds with "Hi, _____," repeating the name and the motion. This continues until all group members have given their names and motions.

Conversation Starter

Once introductions have been made, invite members in your group to share their response to this question: "What small group experiences, if any, have you had in the past, and what do you hope to gain from participating in this small group?" Groups of eight or more participants should break into subgroups of 3-4 so that all may respond and still have time to complete the study session.

Logistics and Covenant

Depending upon whether you are a new or previously formed small group, the amount of time devoted to this portion of the study will vary. "How to Use This Leader Guide" suggests some information that may be appropriate here. Regardless of group history, all groups are encouraged to make a covenant with one another for this six-week study session.

Workbook Review

This week's readings were taken from the Old Testament and focus on God's majesty. Invite members to share their response to the question from Day 2: "What does the word 'fear' mean in Exodus 14:31?" If time allows, ask members to share any insights they gained about God's majesty through the reading of Scripture for the week.

Discussing

SHOW DVD VIDEO

Video Discussion

In the video, Tom Berlin discussed ways in which the wonder of God can be found even in a slug. Can you think of any similar examples?

Share your response to Tom's final question: "Everywhere you look is the majesty of God—if it's all around us, where are you seeing it and where are you missing it?"

Scripture and Discussion

Read aloud Psalm 104 and answer these questions:

1. What is the psalm written about? How is David's psalm similar to or different from the creation story recorded in Genesis 1? (Participants may look back to Genesis 1 as needed. David's psalm is filled with emotion, awe, and worship in response to Creation. Genesis 1 is a factual account of the sequence of Creation.)

2. What elements of nature/creation does David discuss in each section? Verses 2-4? (heaven, wind, rain, lightning) Verses 5-9? (foundations, boundaries, separation of earth and waters, mountains, valleys) Verses 10-18? (abundance of flourishing life: water, birds, animals, plants, food) Verses 19-20? (moon, sun, stars, day and night) Verses 24-26? (oceans and seas, sea creatures)

3. Beyond being Creator, what do verses 27-30 say about God?

4. What realization does David share about God's power and might in verse 32?

 5. As David ponders the wonder of creation, what is his response as recorded in verses 1 and 33-35?

 6. What do verses 10-18 suggest about the holy Creator of the universe? How does knowing that God not only created but also cares and provides for his creatures impact your understanding of God's holiness?

7. Consider verse 24. Why is wisdom a critical component of God's holiness? What is your response to the Christian belief that God is the Creator, mastermind, executive designer, and project manager of the universe? Why?

8. Verses 24-27 suggest that all elements of creation have something in common. What is this? How does this contribute to your understanding of God's holiness?

9. David uses this psalm as a means of sharing that the purpose of nature is to reflect God's glory—to give visibility and insight to the wonder of the invisible God. As a part of God's Creation, what does this suggest about the purpose of your life?

10. Why is reverence an essential character trait in a follower of Christ? How does reverence affect our relationship with God, and what does it do to help us understand and experience God's holiness?

 11. What practical steps can you take this week to be reverent of the Holy God? What daily disciplines or practices will help you to encounter God's holiness more fully?

Closing

Invite group members to share joys and concerns within the group. When all have shared, close with the following prayer or your own.

> *"Holy, holy, holy, Lord God Almighty, all Thy works shall praise Thy name in earth and sky and sea ..."*
> *Surely, Almighty God, there is none beside Thee. Hear our prayers of wonder, awe, and praise, for you alone are God, Creator and Sustainer of the universe. As we consider your holy and perfect nature in the weeks ahead, fill us with your Holy Spirit, that we might be drawn ever closer to you and offer our praise for the inconceivable marvels of your creation. Continue to be at work in us, O Lord, molding us more and more into your likeness. Teach us to be holy, just as you are holy, and hear these prayers that we share with you now. ...*
> *It is in your most holy name we pray. Amen.*

Notes

_____

_____

_____

_____

_____

_____

_____

_____

Week Two

God's Fidelity and My Trust

God's Fidelity and My Trust

Preparing

The goal of this week's session is to show that God's holiness invites our trust. Through the imagery of bridges, the video shows that those things we depend upon, the places and people and things in which we have put our trust, often quite unexpectedly become undependable and uncertain. By contrast, God's fidelity and faithfulness offer a trust that will not disappoint. God is the one thing the believer can depend upon when everything else becomes uncertain.

The Scripture reading offers an example of a believer who placed complete trust in Christ. Jesus states his own amazement at the trust and confidence of the centurion who knew that the power of God was far greater than his own or than any problem he faced. This passage poses a challenge for the reader to examine his or her own faith and trust in Christ.

Faith begins with a step of trust in a God who does not disappoint. The faith journey continues as the believer encounters the holy nature of God: God is steadfast, God is dependable, God is faithful; God can be trusted. No matter where one is on the journey, our Holy God invites us to trust more so that we might experience more fully God's nature and loving provision for us.

Getting Started

Choose one of the following, the icebreaker or the conversation starter, as an introduction to your small-group time. This will allow members to connect with one another and shift their focus to this week's topic.

Icebreaker: Partner Face-Off

Have group members pair up. Partners should stand facing each other a little more than two arm lengths apart, then put their arms in front of them with palms facing forward. While keeping their bodies as straight as possible and their feet in place, they should fall forward, catching each other by the palms of their hands. Challenge the pairs to hold that position for as long as possible, and then push off so they return to a standing position.

Next have everyone take a step back and try it again. Keep moving partners further apart each time to see how long they can be successful at this activity.

Finally, have all the pairs line up together shoulder-to-shoulder with partners still facing each other. Have one line take a half-step to the right so the two sides are staggered. Instruct the group to lean toward one another simultaneously, using one hand to support the original partner and one hand to support the person next to the partner. (End members will be supported by one person only.)

Afterwards ask group members what they learned about trust in this activity. (You may need to prompt and ask what was different when partners moved further apart, or when two people were supporting rather than one.)

Conversation Starter

Ask group members what they are most looking forward to or least looking forward to in the coming week. Why?

Workbook Review

This week's reading included chapters from Luke. Look at Days 2-3 in your workbook. In groups of 3-5, share one Scripture or reflection from which you gained new insight into God's holiness.

Read aloud Luke 5:1-11. Compare yourself to Simon Peter in this story. How is your response to Christ's invitation to trust and follow him similar or dissimilar to the response of Simon Peter?

Discussing

SHOW DVD VIDEO

Video Discussion

1. Where do people tend to place their trust most readily? (Other people, financial security, personal achievement, relationships, health, self, and so on.) Thinking of these things as bridges that people walk across, how have you or others you know experienced one of these bridges being unreliable or even washed away?

2. What is the significance of the boy's building the bridge across the creek?

Scripture and Discussion

Read aloud Luke 7:1-10 and answer the following:

1. What did the centurion want?

2. Contrast what the elders say on behalf of the centurion in verses 4-5 with what he says of himself (relayed by messengers) in verses 6-8. (The elders pleaded on behalf of the centurion because of his status and worth in the community. His friends related that the centurion did not consider himself worthy even to come into Christ's presence. The elders' hope was in the centurion's goodness; the centurion's hope was not in his own power and goodness but in the power of Christ).

3. What did Christ find remarkable about the centurion?

4. In your experience in living the Christian life, why would Christ find the centurion's trust and faith so remarkable? Why is it such a significant difference whether we live with confidence in our own goodness or trust in Christ's power?

5. What do you think the centurion's response would have been if his servant had not been healed? How is our trust in Christ often contingent upon whether we get the things we hope for? Why is it so hard to trust Christ in all things, including sickness and death? What would be your response in this situation?

25

6. Think about a relationship you've had in which a trust was betrayed. Share with the group if this has made it easier or harder for you to trust God. What is the downfall to comparing our relationship with God to our relationships with one another?

7. The Scripture readings for this week referred to lives being made strong through suffering. Think of a time of hardship in your own life or in the life of another Christian and talk about the power that was experienced even in a time of weakness. (Keep in mind that the classic example of power in weakness is Christ's death on the cross. Trusting in a holy God does not mean we are freed from suffering.)

8. In the video, Tom said that we have to choose whether God can be trusted. Reflect and share on the closing question from the video: "Is there a place in your life where God is calling you to take those first trusting steps of faith?"

9. What practical steps can you identify that would strengthen your faith in God and enable you to trust in God's promises with the same confidence as the centurion? Write one of these steps in your workbook as a commitment to yourself to strengthen your faith through positive practice.

Closing

Invite group members to share joys and concerns within the group. When all have shared, close with the following prayer or your own.

> *Lord God, you are a holy God, and have shown yourself throughout the ages to be the God in whom we can place our trust. Help us to have faith like that of the centurion, to remember that in all circumstances, your holiness can be trusted. It is with this faith and trust that we share these concerns, knowing that you are our God who does not disappoint, for you love your children and watch over and care for each one. Hear us as we pray for . . .*
>
> *It is in your holy and trustworthy name we pray. Amen.*

Notes

Week Three

God's Purity and My Humility

God's Purity and My Humility

Preparing

The goal of this week's session is to encounter God's holiness through considering purity. God's purity leads to our humility. The imagery used in this week's video is rain: water in its purest form as it falls from the sky. The Scripture lesson is a parable told by Jesus that compares the prayers of a Pharisee and a tax collector. Purity of heart is taught in this passage by making the distinction between outward righteous display and inward purity of heart. The questions have been designed to generate discussion about God's pure nature, God's desire for purity within us, and the means by which we can experience pure and holy living.

Getting Started

Choose one of the following, either the icebreaker for active learners or the conversation starter for passive learners, as an introduction to your small-group time. This will allow members to connect with one another and shift their focus to this week's topic.

Icebreaker: Human Rainstorm

Explain to your group that by working together you are going to create a rainstorm inside. In order to accomplish this, group members must remain quiet, watch you, and imitate your actions (except that they must stay in one place while you walk). Only when you are in front of someone is that person to begin copying your action, and she or he should continue repeating that action until you are standing in front of the person again.

Begin by rubbing your hands together; move around the group until everyone is imitating this action. Then, returning to where you started, begin the next action, snapping your fingers. Remind the group that they should not begin an action until you move in front of them. Once everyone is snapping, introduce the next action, patting hands on legs. Continue until everyone is doing this. Finally introduce foot-stomping, again moving all the way around the group.

Let the "height" of the storm continue for a brief moment, then reduce the rainstorm by going through the motions in reverse order. Move from stomping to leg-patting to finger-snapping to hand-rubbing to silence. Ask group members to recall a rainstorm and why they remember it so vividly.

Conversation Starter: Purity

Have group members pair up to create a definition of the word *pure* and list five examples of products that advertise themselves as pure (coffee, cosmetics, water, organic food, and so forth). As a group, discuss why consumers are willing to pay for the value of purity in various goods.

Workbook Review

This week's workbook presented a variety of readings from the book of Hebrews. Invite members to share a Scripture or insight that stood out to them this week. If there is time, read aloud Hebrews 7:26-28, 10:19-25, and 12:1-3. Answer the question "What do you understand about the holiness of Christ, and how does keeping your eyes fixed upon Jesus allow you to be made holy through Christ?"

Discussing

SHOW DVD VIDEO

Video Discussion

Rain was used in the video to portray purity. Consider a substance such as pure bottled water that is advertised to be refreshing, revitalizing, and invigorating because of its purity. What percent of contaminants would you be willing to accept in this product and still call it pure? Why? How does thinking about purity and contaminants in substances such as water connect to the holiness of Christ and the holiness that God desires for us?

In the video, Tom Berlin shared that a certain game was a humbling experience and pointed out that step one in encountering God's purity and holiness is to come clean in honesty about ourselves. Why is this such an important step in becoming holy and pure as God desires?

Scripture and Discussion

Read aloud Luke 18:9-14 and answer these questions:

1. To whom does verse 9 indicate Jesus is addressing this parable? Why was this significant enough to note in the Scriptures?

2. What is the difference between the Pharisee and the tax collector in the story that Jesus tells in these verses? Recalling what was discussed last week regarding trust, who in this story is more like the Roman centurion who requested healing for his servant—the Pharisee or the tax collector? Why?

3. Read verses 13-14. What character trait does Christ say will be exalted? Why is humility so significant as we encounter God's holiness?

4. Divide the group into two subgroups to modernize this parable. Give one subgroup the assignment to rewrite the Pharisee's prayer with modern-day language and examples, and give the other subgroup the tax collector's prayer. Allow 3-4 minutes for them to work. Then come back together and have them read their prayers. Ask group members to share what they learned from this exercise.

5. What distinction did Jesus make in the parable between holiness and self-righteousness? What matters more to Christ, the inward heart of a person or outward behavior? It seems logical that people who pursue the spiritual life would see the difference between God's holiness and the state of their own soul. This is not always the case. Discuss why this is not always the case.

6. How easy or hard do you feel it is to be holy? (Although Jesus lived in a holy state of sinless perfection that we can only strive for, it is God's

desire for us to be holy as Christ was holy. The lure of the world and our sinful nature make this daunting. The power of the Holy Spirit and our love for our Lord make it inviting and attainable.)

7. Like the Pharisee in this story, Christ's followers often find it easier to talk about holiness than to be holy! The video states that for us to encounter God's holiness, the impurities of our lives must be filtered out. Discuss your answer to the closing question in the video: "What is God going to have to filter from your character for you to experience the purity God intends for you?"

8. In addition to filtering out the impurities in our lives, what must we be filled with to be more pure and holy as Christ is holy? (God's Holy Spirit, the Word, prayer, time with other disciples to be encouraged and challenged, and so forth)

Closing

Invite group members to share joys and concerns within the group. When all have shared, close with the following prayer or your own.

Almighty, Holy Father of purity, we thank you for your perfect nature, your unblemished existence, which does not coexist with sin. Like the tax collector, help us to be honest about ourselves, our true inward nature, so that we might submit to the power of your Holy Spirit that is our hope to become more of who you want us to be. Forgive us for our self-righteousness and unwillingness to come before you with humility. Help us to showcase less, and seek your mercy more. Forgive us for the many pollutants with which we contaminate your holy nature that longs to dwell within us. With your help, may we recognize those things that are sin and remove them from our lives, and may we seek those things that are holy and pure. As we seek to become your holy people, hear our prayers for those you love. . . .
It is in your most holy name we pray. Amen.

Notes

God's Authority and My Obedience

God's Authority and My Obedience

Preparing

The goal of this week's session is to encounter God's holiness through considering obedience. God's authority leads to our obedience. The imagery used in this week's video comes from words inscribed on Washington, D.C., government buildings. Just as the decisions and rulings made within these buildings have authority over the lives of U.S. citizens, so does God have authority over the lives of Christians. Christians recognize God's ultimate authority over all things, including their own lives, and respond with obedience. They come to understand that God's way is always the best way, and begin to seek God's direction more and more. The Scripture lessons included examine the authority by which Christ sends out the disciples and the authority by which he calms a storm. The questions have been designed to deepen our understanding of divine power and authority so that as Jesus' disciples we can claim God's power and authority in our own lives and reflect God's kingdom here on earth.

Getting Started

Choose one of the following, either the icebreaker for active learners or the conversation starter for passive learners, as an introduction to your small-group time. This will allow members to connect with one another and shift their focus to this week's topic.

Icebreaker: Interpretive Ripping

Explain that you will be giving specific instructions for an activity and will not answer questions, so as not to confuse the task sequence. Give everyone, including yourself, an 8½x11–inch sheet of paper and tell them to close their eyes. Then give the following instructions: "Fold the paper in half. Rip off a corner. Fold the paper in half. Rip off a corner. Fold the paper in half. Rip off a corner. Open your eyes." As group members view the varied creations resulting from the same directions, ask, "What made following these simple directions so complex?" and "How is our response to God's direction for our lives somewhat similar to this activity?"

Conversation Starter

Ask participants to share their thoughts on why individuals can know what is best for them, but not make that choice. Give examples of food to eat, need for daily exercise, sleep requirements etc. Often we attribute poor choices to not knowing better, but to what can we attribute poor choices to when we are fully informed?

Workbook Review

This week the workbook presented a variety of readings from the book of Romans. Share your responses to the question from Day 3, "Why is obedience to God so important to Paul?" If time permits, ask group members to share a Scripture or insight that reveals what they have come to understand about obedience as an attribute of holiness.

Discussing

SHOW DVD VIDEO

Video Discussion

The phrases shown on the buildings evoke a common cause or goal greater than any individual to be served. What would be the benefit of having a motto for your own life? What place would God and God's will have in such a motto? (In the video Tom said, "It is easy to forget. It is easy to forget who you are to serve." Later he stated, "We get it out of order. We see ourselves as the most important being in the universe. Our issues are *the* issues. Our desires are *the* desires. Our problems are *the* problems. Prayers that once placed us at the center of God's will become requests that ask God to center on our will.")

Drawing upon the imagery in the video, what does it mean to you to be obedient to God and allow God to be the architect of your life? (Tom said, "Whenever we have an encounter with God's authority, it produces respect that leads to our obedience. We see that we are finite and God is infinite. We are limited in knowledge and God is all-knowing. We are frail and God is powerful.")

Scripture and Discussion

Read aloud Luke 8:22-25 and answer these questions:

1. Where were the disciples and Jesus in verses 22-23? What was Jesus doing? Why were the disciples fearful?

2. What did Jesus do when the disciples awoke him and he saw their fear? What did he reveal about himself when he rebuked the waves?

3. What was Jesus' question to the disciples in verse 25? What did the disciples then realize about Jesus?

Read aloud Luke 9:1-6 and answer these questions:

4. What did Jesus give to the disciples in verse 1? What did he command them to do in verse 2?

5. What is the significance of the instructions Christ gives the disciples in verses 4-5?

6. What was the response of the disciples to Christ's instructions in verse 6?

Read aloud Luke 9:18-27 and answer these questions:

7. What question does Jesus ask in verse 18? What is the disciple's response in verse 19?

8. What is the next question Jesus asks in verse 20? Why is it significant that Christ asked the question "Who do *you* say that I am?"

41

9. How do the activities the disciples were sent out to perform (Luke 9:2) compare with what they had witnessed in Christ? Luke 9:6 reports that they were successful. By whose authority were they equipped to accomplish such things? Why is this important information for a modern-day disciple of Christ?

10. Why must every disciple, both long ago and today, answer Jesus' question "Who do you say that I am?" What impact does the answer "You are the Christ" have upon one's life? (For example, confirmation is an opportunity for young people within the church to answer the question "Who is Jesus?" Separating themselves from what family members and/or friends believe, each confirmand individually considers and answers this question. This is a critical experience within the life of the person, for faith in Christ becomes his or her own choice.)

11. Explain the paradox shared by Christ in Luke 9:24: "For whoever wants to save their life will lose it, but whoever loses their life for me will save it."

12. Share if or when you have answered Christ's question "Who do you say that I am?" In light of your response, consider Tom's closing question: "What words are being chiseled in your life, and what do those words say about who you serve?" Take a few moments and write a life motto, a guiding statement that describes your life or the motto you hope will describe your life from this day forward.

Closing

Invite group members to share joys and concerns within the group. When all have shared, close with the following prayer or your own.

Almighty, Holy God, whose authority expands both heaven and earth, we bow before you. You speak and the waves are calmed. With just the touch of your hand or a word from your lips, miracle upon miracle has been bestowed. Teach us to obey you, Holy God. Guide us in your ways. As we profess you to be Lord over all, come and be Lord of our lives. As we truly yield ourselves to you, take authority over our lives and use them for the furthering of your kingdom. Send us forth as you did your disciples of long ago with all power and authority to perform all that you would have us do. As we seek to become your holy and obedient people, hear our prayers for those you love: . . .

It is in your most holy and all-powerful name we pray. Amen.

Notes

_____

_____

_____

_____

_____

_____

_____

_____

_____

_____

_____

_____

**Week
Five**

God's Righteousness and My Work for Justice

God's Righteousness and My Work for Justice

Preparing

The goal of this week's session is to show that God's righteousness leads us to work for justice. The video is much like watching the news most nights—poverty, abuse, oppression, and inhumane conditions are prevalent in our world. While we see these images with our own eyes and in our minds know that they exist, we are often blind to it all. We worship God, we talk about our own transformation, and we talk of our hope of eternal life, but we never see the world any differently. We never see the world as Jesus saw the world. We don't realize that as God's holy and righteous people, we are God's helpers and are called to reach out to the needy world we live in and do our part to work for the justice that is God's will.

This is what the ministry of Jesus is all about. He came to earth to make the world right with God. He knew the desire of God and knew the standard God wanted maintained. When he came to this world, he could see how far the world had strayed from God's will. Jesus came to do something about it and to show us true righteousness. He taught in his ministry, "The spirit of the Lord is on me, / because he has anointed me / to proclaim good news to the poor. / He has sent me to proclaim freedom for the prisoners / and recovery of sight for the blind, / to set the oppressed free, / to proclaim the year of the Lord's favor" (Luke 4:18-19).

God's desire in the world is to restore peace wherever it has been broken. As disciples of Jesus, we are to do God's will. What is it we are supposed to do? John the Baptist gives us some guidance: If you have an extra coat, share with the person who doesn't own one; if you are a soldier, don't exploit your power; be ethical in your business; don't falsely accuse others (Luke 3:11-14). After encountering God's righteousness, we will see the world differently. We will be willing servants of the Lord and seek to live like Jesus, reflecting the Kingdom of God, which brings peace to the world as well as to our own hearts.

Getting Started

Choose one of the following, either the icebreaker for active learners or the conversation starter for passive learners, as an introduction to your small-group time. This will allow members to connect with one another and shift their focus to this week's topic.

Icebreaker: Rock, Paper, Scissors

Divide the group into pairs. As the facilitator, you will be the caller and the judge. When you say, "1, 2, 3, go," participants in each pair will hold out one of three symbols with their hands: flat hand = paper; fist = rock; pointer and middle fingers extended in a V shape = scissors. A winner will be declared in each pair according to the following standard: Rock takes scissors, paper takes rock, scissors take paper. Play three rounds with paired groups, with the best out of three being the winner.

Then divide the entire group into two teams. Play the same game, except instead of pairs, play between the two teams. Each team will have to come to a quick consensus of what symbol to throw. Again, play three rounds, with the best of three being the winner. Then discuss: "Did you ever feel the game was unfair? Why? Do you credit yourself or circumstances with your win or loss? Why?"

Conversation Starter: "That's Not Fair!"

Recall and share a recent experience in which you or someone you know was treated unfairly. How did you respond? How important is "fairness" to you? Are you a "justice seeker"? Why or why not?

Workbook Review

This week's readings focus on God's righteousness. Recognizing God's righteousness can lead to a willingness to work for justice in our fallen world. Invite members to share a Scripture or insight from the week's readings that spoke to them about their desire to be righteous and work for justice. If there is time, read Isaiah 51:1-8 and answer the question from Day 4, "What is the connection between God's righteousness and our work for justice?"

Discussing

SHOW DVD VIDEO

Video Discussion

What do you think is the meaning of the camera in the video? (Images of the needs in this world are readily available to us, but just because we see them doesn't mean we always do something about it.)

Tom Berlin ended the video by saying, "Look around you. There are thousands of problems in this world crying out for justice, limitless opportunities." Discuss his final questions: "Which one of those has your attention, and what are you going to do about it?"

Scripture and Discussion

Read aloud Luke 16:19-31 and answer the following questions:

1. What is the distinguishing factor between the life of Lazarus and the life of the rich man?

2. What happened to Lazarus when he died? And the rich man?

3. The rich man pleaded twice with Abraham. What was the rich man's second request?

4. What was Abraham's response to his plea? (If people's minds are closed and Scripture is rejected, no evidence—not even a resurrection—will change them.)

5. What was the problem with the rich man's life?

6. On Day 1 in your workbook for the week, you were asked to find the definition of *righteousness* in the dictionary. Discuss your understanding of righteousness. (Webster defines *righteousness* as acting in accord with divine or moral law.)

7. Read Psalm 96:10-13 aloud. What does the psalmist tell us the world will be like when the Kingdom of God comes?

8. Read Luke 4:18-19 aloud. What does Christ say about the Kingdom of God? (In the New Testament, Jesus is recognized as the Messiah. The Messiah came, but not the Kingdom of God did not arrive as the Old Testament believers thought it would.)

9. What did believers come to learn from Jesus and his ministry? How does this differ from what Old Testament believers thought? (The Kingdom of God is embodied in Christ. Both John the Baptist and Jesus proclaimed that the Kingdom was near. The parables that compare the Kingdom to a seed that is growing or yeast in dough convey that while the Kingdom is near, it has not yet come in its fullness. The advancement of God's Kingdom on earth is therefore made complete through Christ's disciples.)

10. What does "The Kingdom of God is near" mean for Christ's followers today? (We are the hope of God. God empowered us with the gift of the Holy Spirit, and Jesus explained that it is up to God's righteous and holy people—us—to bring the Kingdom of Heaven to earth. We are the angels of change and agree to do God's will here on earth while we wait in joyful hope for the coming of our Savior.)

11. Read Luke 4:18-19 again, inserting a member's name each time Christ is referred to in the passage (for example, "The Spirit of the Lord is upon Joe, because he has anointed Joe to preach good news," and so on). What impact does this have on your ability to see the world and on your willingness to work for justice?

12. Encountering God's holy righteousness leads to a deeper understanding of God's will for the world and what we are called to do. After the discussion today, what is God inviting you to do? Where is God inviting you to participate in the work?

13. If there is time, have members share ways in which they are seeking and advancing God's kingdom with their work for justice. Come up with other possible ways that they could help in our world.

Closing

Invite group members to share joys and concerns within the group. When all have shared, close with the following prayer or your own.

Holy and most righteous Maker and Ruler of the universe, who in the beginning created and ordered our world, you are most worthy of our praise. As we consider the intricate wonder of your creation, and the careful means by which you have ordered all things, our hearts are heavy as we consider the chaos and disorder that marks our humanity. We come before you humbly seeking and yearning for your righteousness to reign within our lives. By the power of your Holy Spirit, may we see the world as you see it and may we be responsive to your persistent invitation to be a part of your work in redeeming the world. Show us where we may be a part of what you are blessing, and make us ever ready to help you work for justice in our broken world. Just as we seek order and peace in our world, so do we lift up these names for your holy power in their lives. . . .

It is in your righteous, powerful, and holy name we pray. Amen.

Notes

_____

_____

_____

_____

God's Graciousness and My Love of Others

God's Graciousness and My Love of Others

Preparing

The goal of this week's session is to consider how God's abundant grace can free us to love others. This grace is freely given by a loving and holy God and is based not upon our own merit or favor but simply on God's abundant generosity in bestowing it upon us. The video uses a prison to illustrate that our lives often are bound by the burdens of sin and feelings of anger, frustration, or hurt. Receiving God's grace and experiencing God's graciousness are essential to our freedom from traits that make us unholy. As we encounter God's holiness through grace, we often find that God's graciousness toward us leads to our greater love and grace for others. Not only are we set free from our burdens, but in turn we are able to bless others with the same grace God has extended to us. The holy God entrusts us with grace to reflect the Kingdom here on earth.

In the Parable of the Good Samaritan, it is important to explain some of the background for this story. Jews and Samaritans practiced open hostility toward one another during this time of Jesus' ministry. Jews viewed Samaritans as half-breeds, both physically and spiritually. The fact that the Samaritan was the one to help the Jewish man who was left for dead on the side of the road has greater significance when this context is understood. This act of grace illustrates Jesus' point that God's love shows no boundaries and our love for others can follow this example.

Getting Started

Choose one of the following, either the icebreaker for active learners or the conversation starter for passive learners, as an introduction to your small-group time. This will allow members to connect with one another and shift their focus to this week's topic.

Icebreaker: Object Definitions

Take various random items—such as an ink pen, a clothespin, a garbage bag, a flashlight, an eraser, a bottle of cleanser, soap, a "Get Out of Jail Free" card from a Monopoly game, a marker, and so forth—and place these items on a table or on the floor in the center of the group.

Instruct the group to think for a moment about the word *grace*. Then ask each participant to consider the attributes of the objects displayed and select an item that is reflective of their individual understanding of the word. Participants don't have to actually pick up the items, as more than one member might choose the same object (though they may have different reasons for doing so). Have members explain their choices, one at a time, to open the session's discussion about grace.

Conversation Starter: Grace in Common

As a large group, or in various small groups, discover what common experiences of grace the group members have shared. Examples might include getting a warning rather than a ticket, speeding past an officer but not being pulled over, being late but still being the first one to arrive, and so on. Use this as an entry conversation to the theme of this session, God's grace.

Workbook Review

This week's readings focus on grace and the connections we find between grace, love, and freedom. Invite members to share a Scripture or insight from the week's reading that spoke to them about grace.

If there is time, read Galatians 5:1-6 and answer the question from Day 5, "For Paul, what is the connection between freedom and love?"

Discussing

SHOW DVD VIDEO

Video Discussion

What is the significance of Tom Berlin being in a jail cell?

Tom started by saying that he was envious of God's heart because it was full of grace. What do you admire about God's heart? In what ways do you desire to gain the heart of God?

Scripture and Discussion

Read aloud Luke 10:25-37 and answer the following questions:

1. In verses 25-29, Jesus is asked two questions. What are they?

2. Jesus answers the man with the Parable of the Good Samaritan. Why is it significant that the Samaritan be the one who helped the injured man, a Jew? (See "Preparing" above for information relevant to this question.)

3. Scripture does not say why the priest and the Levite passed by without helping the injured man. Discuss possible reasons for their lack of action. Share an experience in which you may have acted like the priest or Levite. What justifications do we often give for our own lack of compassion?

4. How does the parable answer the question "Who is my neighbor?"

5. What is your understanding of grace? In the video, Tom mentioned ways we may have experienced grace. Share other ways you may have received God's grace. Why has God been so abundant with grace?

6. On a scale of 1 to 10, rank the measure of grace you've received in your life. If God's grace cannot be earned, purchased, or negotiated, how can we receive it? (Often our decision to accept grace hinges on the degree of humility we possess. While we can choose to accept grace or not, it is unmistakable that the more aware we are of God's grace the more likely we are to extend grace to others).

7. Beyond the pity mentioned in the Bible passage, the Samaritan showed compassion towards the injured man. Discuss the difference between pity and compassion. (Both conjure feelings of sorrow for someone, but compassion adds a desire to alleviate the suffering with action.) God does not pity us but has compassion for all of us children. God's love shows no boundaries. As a group, discuss ways in which God's compassion for you reveals grace in your own life.

8. Tom ends the video with a question: "What do you need to do to set your heart free?" Share your responses to this question.

9. When we experience God's grace, we often feel compelled to extend grace to others, not because we feel we have to but because it brings us joy. (Jesus' ministry is all about experiencing God's grace. Jesus mirrored the holiness and goodness of God by extending the grace that had been given him to others. In each case, he was a blessing to others and his life became a blessing.) Share an experience in which you extended grace to another and discovered that through giving the gift of grace, you in turn received the blessing of God.

Closing

Take a moment to pose the following questions to your group before praying:

What is your hope about yourself as you close the pages of this study having learned about Six Ways We Encounter God? What do you hope to retain and put into practice?

Invite group members to share joys and concerns within the group. When all have shared, close with the following prayer or your own.

Holy God of abundant grace, we come before you
humbled by the knowledge of the generosity of your grace
and mercy. As we are aware of the measure of grace we
have experienced in our own lives, help us to extend
grace to others. Particularly, God, help us to be holy as

you are holy, and to be willing and ready to extend grace and mercy to those for whom it is hardest to give. Keep us ever mindful of all that we have received from you so that we too might be generous in our response to others. It is with your holy grace in mind that we lift these names to you now, asking for your grace and mercy in their lives as well. . . .

It is in your holy and abundantly gracious name we pray. Amen.

Notes

_____

_____

_____

_____

_____

_____

_____

_____

_____

_____

_____

_____

_____

Notes

_____

_____

_____

_____

_____

_____

_____

_____

_____

_____

_____

_____

_____

_____

_____

_____

_____

_____

_____

_____

_____

_____

Notes